DISCOVERING PRAYER

Everyone prays, at least occasionally. But what are we doing when we pray?

This book is to help people understand prayer. It is a guide to effective and enjoyable ways of praying.

DISCOVERING PRAYER

Andrew Knowles

A LION MANUAL
Oxford · Batavia · Sydney

Text copyright © 1985 Andrew Knowles
This edition copyright © 1993 Lion Publishing

The author asserts the moral right
to be identified as the author of this work

Published by
Lion Publishing plc
Sandy Lane West, Oxford, England
ISBN 0 7459 2644 4
Lion Publishing
1705 Hubbard Avenue, Batavia, Illinois 60510, USA
ISBN 0 7459 2644 4
Albatross Books Pty Ltd
PO Box 320, Sutherland, NSW 2232, Australia
ISBN 0 7324 0656 0

First edition 1985
Reprinted 1989
This edition 1993

A catalogue record for this book
is available from the British Library

**Library of Congress Cataloging-in-
Publication Data**
Knowles, Andrew
    Discovering prayer / Andrew Knowles
    ISBN 0-7459-2644-4
    1. Prayer—Christianity. I. Title.
  BV210.2.K57 1993   92-44876
  248.3'2—dc20   CIP

Acknowledgments
Bible quotations are from the *Good News Bible*,
copyright American Bible Society, New York, 1966,
1971 and 4th edition 1976, published by the Bible
Societies/HarperCollins, with permission.

Printed in Slovenia

CONTENTS

Discovering Prayer   7

We are all of us closer to praying than we sometimes realize. At the key moments and problem
times of life, we easily begin to pray.

Discovering God   11

When we pray, it helps to know who we're talking
to. God is not just a picture in our imagination. He
has shown us what he is like—in the Bible, and
supremely in Jesus.

Discovering Jesus   29

Jesus prayed a great deal. And he taught his
followers to pray. His teaching highlights prayer as
the focus of the whole Christian life.

Discovering the Spirit   57

Prayer is a spiritual activity, and God has given his
Holy Spirit to help us to pray. So rather than
struggling to do something that goes against the
grain, we need to let him take us up into prayer.

Discovering Ourselves   71

Prayer needs to be part of our ordinary human life.
As everything we are and do becomes open to God,
all that is deepest in us can be turned into prayer.
But how can we begin?

1

DISCOVERING PRAYER

God loves us. His motive in making us was love.
His greatest longing is that we should get to know
him, come to love him, enjoy his company.
And when we talk to God or listen to him, head to
head, heart to heart, this is prayer.

EVERYBODY DOES IT

We all pray.

As we go into an examination; as our plane taxies along the runway ready for take-off; as the medical orderlies wheel us into the operating theatre; as we frantically search the superstore for a missing toddler ...

In all the emergencies of life, prayer is never far from our lips. Never mind if we are hardened atheists the rest of the time. The fact is that when we need that extra help, or the hunt is on for someone to blame, we turn to God.

And this is true of every culture in the world. The West watched in amazement when dead leaders of the communist bloc were buried with full religious ceremony. Clearly two generations of official and military atheism had failed to stamp out a deep desire to turn to God and commit loved ones to his almighty care.

But we don't always feel such a need to pray. In some ways humankind has outgrown the need for such a prop. Modern science and technology have done so much to make our lives both safer and more comfortable. Advances in medicine have eased our aches and pains and eliminated many serious diseases. If we suffer from depression or nourish inconvenient hang-ups, the psychiatrist will surely help.

All in all, we can probably cut God out of nearly every area of our lives. We simply don't need him any more. As for asking for our daily bread, we have plenty in the freezer already, thank you very much. And anyway we prefer cake.

If this is our view of life, we're in deep trouble. Technology has taken us over, and we're no longer in touch with the real world at all.

What can we say when we find that the house of our dreams, filled to overflowing with precious possessions, turns out to be the coldest of prisons, because all our money couldn't buy the smallest shred of love? Where can we go when we've read all the agony columns, consulted all the advisors and taken all the pills, and still can't find peace of mind?

The things that matter most—love, peace, freedom and dignity—simply don't come from the supermarket. They spring only from God himself. They are the fruits of prayer.

We all pray when we're desperate, just as we all run when we need to catch a bus. But if our friendship with God is really to grow, we need to give him our full attention. We need to spend time with him. We need to adjust to him—letting him change us in many ways, and making some changes ourselves.

When we spend time with God, we get to be like him. The changes in us may not be instant or dramatic; it is far more likely that they will be gradual and take place over a period of time. The most welcome change will be that God

Parents long that their baby will have the best possible life. This longing is very close to prayer

will give us peace of mind. He will also assure us of his love, and give us a new ability to love those around us. Other people may notice that we are developing an inner strength, that we are more certain of our direction in life, and that we have the resources to cope not just with everyday hassles but with the really testing crises that come our way.

This kind of spiritual stability is God's gift. We can neither buy it nor earn it, and there is nothing we have done to deserve it. All we can do is humbly turn to God and ask him to start his new work in our lives.

From here we can embark on the adventure of life with God. We need to practise spending time with him. We can discover more about him by reading the Bible and by talking to other Christians. And we need to be patient with ourselves. We don't run a hundred metres in under ten seconds simply by reading a book on jogging, or by carrying with us a photo of Carl Lewis. No more do we develop our friendship with God by mastering a method or purchasing a system.

Prayer isn't a method anyway. It's a way of life.

The search for God is worldwide and takes many forms

In Jerusalem, Jews pray at the Wailing Wall.

In Cairo, Muslims pray at the El Azhar Mosque.

A group of Christians meet informally to pray

DISCOVERING GOD

To discover prayer, we have first to discover God.
And this means turning ourselves inside-out.
It means we have to let God be our God—not just
Lord of the universe, majestic and remote, but Lord
of our lives. We must get out of the limelight, vacate
the stage, and make our hearts his royal throne.

DEAR WHO?

God knows and loves us, and we in turn want to know and love him. But what is he like? What can we call him?

He is our Creator

The very first words of the Bible are: 'In the beginning, when God created the universe...' Without God's creative and powerful love, we would never have been brought into being. Everything we are and everything we enjoy comes from him. Wherever we look we see the evidence of his creativity—from the vast galaxies of deep space to the scales on the wings of a butterfly.

The Bible says that God brought us into being as part of his plan for the whole cosmos. And if we are part of his purpose, then we want to enter wholeheartedly into all that he has in store for us. We want to thank God for his gift of life and for the exquisite experience of our existence. We want to praise and reverence him as our Creator God. We want to serve him as our Lord.

He is different from us

We can discover God's creation and wonder at it, but we can never 'see' God himself. The Bible reveals that God is 'spirit'—eternal, invisible, powerful, and ever-present. Above all, God is 'holy'—that means he is utterly different from us in his

intense purity and infinite power.

We can only know this holy God because he lets himself be known. There is no way we can locate him, analyze him and catalogue him as though he were some interesting specimen from outer space. Instead, we abandon ourselves to his greatness. We adore him.

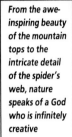

From the awe-inspiring beauty of the mountain tops to the intricate detail of the spider's web, nature speaks of a God who is infinitely creative

If we try to define God, get our minds round him and take possession of him, he will always elude us. But if we put ourselves in his way and let him take our lives in his hands, then we will find ourselves possessed by him.

Throw out the old pictures!

God is not an old man in the sky. It seems that any cartoonist wanting to depict God draws him as an elderly gent perched on a fluffy cloud, keeping a sharp lookout for wrongdoers and with a pile of thunderbolts handy. The idea goes back to the Greek god Zeus (the Romans called him Jupiter), and this image has somehow been handed down to us, pausing only to pick up Santa Claus on the way.

Of course, it's natural enough for us to think of God as 'old'. We can't easily grasp that he's eternal and so we simply think of him as having been around a long time. Again, we naturally think of him as being 'up there' because he's infinitely superior to us—and in any case, if he 'sees' everything he must presumably do so from a suitable vantage point. If we are to come to the Living God as he really is, we will almost certainly have to discard some of the mental pictures we have had of him in the past.

God is not an invisible policeman. Perhaps we think of God as an ever-present law-keeper—always on our back, constantly updating the files on our guilty secrets and stacking video-recordings of our lives on the shelves of heaven ready for slow-motion replay on Judgment Day.

If this is our picture of God, then we're confusing him with our conscience. We all have a conscience—a sensitive internal compass which continually monitors whether we're doing right or wrong. But it has to be said that our conscience is also moulded by our culture and upbringing. We can get to feel 'bad' about almost anything, from eating meat on Fridays to watching a film on a sunny afternoon. On the other hand, our conscience may have got badly blunted, perhaps by involvement with a particular circle of friends, and we may have come to believe that 'anything goes'.

Either way, it makes no sense to amplify the voice of our own conscience and call it God. Whether our inner voice demands perfection or gives no

moral guidelines at all, it's obviously inadequate as a revelation of God's truth.

God is not your Mum and Dad. For most of us, our first memories of comfort and belonging (and of being disciplined!) are bound up with the early years spent with our parents. The love and care of our mothers and fathers was invaluable to us, and we owe them our lives.

Nevertheless, there is no such thing as the perfect parent! Parents can foster too great a dependence on them, so that their children are 'tied to their apron strings' for ever. They may be negligent—too busy pursuing their own goals in life to have time for their children. Either parent may be a source of unending demands that a child tries hard to fulfil; or their standards may be variable and their reactions unpredictable and violent.

So when we turn to God, we may bring a whole bundle of confused needs and longings, hopes and fears, which are all to do with the way we were treated when we were young. To hear that God is 'like a father' may fill us with dread if our own father was a tyrant. But the description of God as 'Father' is the best way of saying that we belong to him and that he is interested in us and loves us. So let's keep what matters and discard the rest.

But there are dangers if we carry on thinking of God in this way. 'Old' can too easily carry the notion that God is now absent-minded, short-sighted, and in every way behind the times. This is a gross misrepresentation of the Living God—the God who is eternally alive, who was never young and will never be old—the God who simply is.

God is not the missing piece. Some people think of God as a little part of life that they can't understand or control. His heyday was in the past when his help was indispensable in all matters from having babies and growing crops to travelling safely and warding off plague. In some countries he may well be needed for all these things today. But where civilization is well established we know better (or so that argument goes). With so much of life's jigsaw

successfully pieced together, there is little room for God at all. He is left to fill those spaces caused by the loss of a loved one, our longing for a sense of purpose, or our need for help in extreme emergency.

Such a view of God has promoted ourselves to manage the universe, with God as an extra pair of hands if needed. It totally ignores the fact that all we are and all we have comes from him, and that without his continuing power and creativity our world—and indeed the whole universe—would collapse into chaos and revert to nothingness! God is far from being the part of a jigsaw we haven't yet worked out: he is the Creator and Sustainer of the whole of life from black holes to gluons. We are kidding ourselves if we think we can give him notice to quit.

God is not a friendly wizard. We have the idea that God is some kind of amiable magician or genie who can smooth our passage through life and avert disaster if only we learn how to conjure him up. We may have our own favourite example of how he has intervened to help us. And perhaps our

religion is very much geared to keeping in touch with this useful friend and staying on the right side of him. Do we wear a special charm or trinket (or carry one in the car) to help this handy God to locate us in times of need?

This is a very false picture of Almighty God. It assumes all the time that we are centre-stage and his is a walk-on part. He exists for our benefit, fortunate to be included as a footnote to our lives. Put like that, we can see our mistake. Of course God knows our needs; he wants to help us and he can. But he does so because we are his children and he loves us, and not because he is a celestial fixer we have learned to manipulate.

HOW DOES IT WORK?

All the great Christians who have ever lived have testified to the value of prayer.

The eighteenth-century preacher George Whitefield was up at four in the morning to pray. (Mind you, he was in bed by ten at night.) His contemporary John Wesley was convinced that 'God does nothing but in answer to prayer', and he spent two hours each day seeking God's blessing on his work.

The formidable Martin Luther, who pioneered the Protestant Reformation and changed the course of German history, depended on prayer for the direction of his life.

If I fail to spend two hours in prayer each morning, the devil gets the victory throughout the day. I have so much business I cannot get on without spending three hours daily in prayer.

The English reformer, William Wilberforce, would have agreed wholeheartedly. Despite the enormous pressures of public life, including many decades spent fighting for the abolition of slavery, he habitually gave three hours of each day to prayer.

But what happens when we pray? Is it that we give God ideas he hasn't thought of? Surely not! Is it that we finally persuade him to do something he's been meaning to get around to? Again, the very idea seems ludicrous. It is we who need

persuading to do good, not God.

In prayer, we get down to business with God.

The agenda of his kingdom becomes our agenda. We ask to see the world through his eyes, to engage in life with something of his deep compassion and self-giving love. It's not that we change God's mind when we pray, but that he changes ours.

In prayer, we're privileged to work with God.

As William Temple once said, 'When I pray coincidences happen; when I don't they don't.' It's almost as though difficult problems and situations can be 'broken down' by prayer. Or as if they are in some way 'porous' and can be permeated and changed by the invading power of God.

And prayer is indispensable to our own spiritual development.

William Carey said, 'Prayer— secret, fervent, believing prayer— lies at the root of all personal godliness.' This isn't the godliness that arises from seeking to manipulate God, or presenting him with a list of our daily requirements. Rather it's a godliness which springs from sharing our lives with Jesus. We spend time with him. Our friendship develops and grows. We get to love the people and things that he loves and we come to hate the things he hates.

We may begin our life of prayer

with a sense of making a big effort to get through to God and win his attention and response. But before long we discover that prayer is not all 'give'. In fact by far the greater part of prayer is in learning how to receive.

Praying for others will always be a demanding experience. It means that we put ourselves in their position, feel their pain, explore their dilemma. And then we stand with them and plead for them in the light and warmth of God's love.

We may often feel that very little is being achieved, and that we're really wasting our time. But sincere prayer is never wasted. The only waste is if we spend time wondering whether our prayer is being heard by God, or whether it's doing any good. There is a 'pain threshold' in prayer for others, and we need to learn how to surmount it. When we press on through the barriers of impatience and unbelief, we come through to a vantage-point from which we can pray with greater faith, freedom and vision.

Being with God

When you have a great friend you may plan to spend a time with him and be careful not to miss it. The use of the time is unlikely to be planned, but within the time news may be shared, requests may be made, regrets or gratitude may be spoken, and minds be exchanged, sometimes by talking and listening, and sometimes with little word or gesture . . .

To be with God wondering, that is adoration. To be with God gratefully, that is thanksgiving. To be with God ashamed, that is contrition. To be with God with others on the heart, that is intercession. The secret is the quest of God's presence: 'Thy face, Lord, will I seek.'

MICHAEL RAMSEY

WHAT STOPS US?

If God is so real and prayer is such a privilege, whatever stops us? The answer is easy: we don't want to start.

Something in us naturally recoils from prayer. The presence and peace and power of God in our lives is a lovely thought, but we don't want to spend time on it now. It's not half as exciting as the soap opera on television, and by no means as urgent as the call we plan to make at the end of the programme.

But beneath the surface of these immediate excuses, there is a vast reservoir of self-centredness and hostility to God. The early chapters of the Bible tell how the very first man and woman disobeyed God and started to avoid him: 'That evening they heard the Lord God walking in the garden, and they hid from him among the trees.'

Like Adam and Eve, we realize that to meet with God face to face will plunge us into crisis. We can't in any way claim to be open to God while at the same time nursing resentments, bearing grudges and generally insisting on having our own way all the time.

The Galilean fisherman, Simon Peter, had it right. He fell on his knees in front of Jesus and said, 'Go away from me, Lord! I am a sinful man!'

Why don't we pray? Because we're on the run from God. We've a hundred and one things we want to get on with, and we're scared he'll call for a change in our priorities. We have a thousand guilty secrets we want to hide, and we know he'll see right through us.

In the face of all this, there is only one thing to do. We have to put on the brakes, step out in the open, and say, 'Lord, help me to want to pray.'

There are a million and one things to keep us busy. We need to ask God to help us to want to pray

GOD'S GIFT TO US

The first and best reason for prayer is that God has invited us to approach him. If we wait until we feel like praying, or are driven to it by the urgency of our needs, then we miss the point.

In one of the psalms, God says: 'Call to me when trouble comes; I will save you, and you will praise me.'

These words were written nearly 3,000 years ago and yet God's invitation is as real and fresh as a newsflash. When we're in trouble we can turn to him. He will surely save us, and we will have yet another glorious reason to praise him.

Then again, prayer is one of the weapons God has given us in the face of temptation. On the night of his arrest, Jesus said to his disciples, 'Keep watch and pray that you will not fall into temptation'. When our imagination is bounding away into immoral fantasies, or when we're failing to control what we look at, listen to, or say ... When we're really stretched on the rack of greed, jealousy or lust, how wonderful that we can pray! We can reduce the pressure instantly by simply shouting out to God for help.

Prayer is also the right response to the times in which we live. When Jesus described the state of the world between his first and second coming —from the day of his physical departure from the earth until the unknown date when he will powerfully reappear on the world scene—he spoke of cosmic upheaval, natural disasters, false religious leaders and recurring wars. In the midst of all this, Jesus told his followers not to be paralyzed with panic, nor to take refuge in feasting, drinking and other pleasures of the body. Instead he urged prayer:

Be on the alert and pray always that you will have the strength to go safely through all those things that will happen and to stand before the Son of Man.

Paul the apostle also encouraged Christians to surround all they did with prayer. He wrote to the Thessalonians:

Be joyful always, pray at all times, be thankful in all circumstances. This is what God wants from you in your life in union with Christ Jesus.

God is everywhere

Lord, you have examined me and you
  know me.
You know everything I do;
  from far away you understand all my
    thoughts.
You see me, whether I am working or
  resting;
  you know all my actions.
Even before I speak,
  you already know what I will say.
You are all around me on every side;
  you protect me with your power.
Your knowledge of me is too deep;
  it is beyond my understanding.
Where could I go to escape from you?
  Where could I get away from your
    presence?
If I went up to heaven, you would be
  there;
  If I lay down in the world of the dead,
    you would be there.
If I flew away beyond the east
  or lived in the farthest place in the west,
you would be there to lead me,
  you would be there to help me.
I could ask the darkness to hide me
  or the light round me to turn into night,
but even darkness is not dark for you,
  and the night is as bright as the day.
  Darkness and light are the same to you.

You created every part of me;
  you put me together in my mother's
    womb.
I praise you because you are to be feared;
  all you do is strange and wonderful.
  I know it with all my heart.
When my bones were being formed,
  carefully put together in my mother's
    womb,
when I was growing there in secret,
  you knew that I was there—
  you saw me before I was born.

The days allotted to me
  had all been recorded in your book,
  before any of them ever began.
O God, how difficult I find your thoughts;
  how many of them there are!
If I counted them, they would be more
  than the grains of sand.
  When I awake, I am still with you.

PSALM 139

SEEING THE WORLD WHOLE

We live in a complex, fast-moving and bewildering world—a world several stages removed from reality.

We buy food at the superstore without giving a thought to how it was produced or processed. We drive vehicles which most of us couldn't make or maintain, and rely on communication systems we don't begin to understand. All in all, our lives are the end-product of a vast number of interconnected processes, nearly all of which we take for granted.

How vulnerable we are! A power cut, a radiation leak or the spread of a new virus, and suddenly we realize that our so-called civilization is precariously balanced.

It is vital and healthy to see this world as a whole. It's good to commit ourselves to God's plan for our life in this world. But there is only one vantage-point from which we can see the world this way, and that is prayer. There is only one channel through which God can bring about wholeness in our lives, and that is prayer.

Prayer enables us to stand back and see our fragmented world as a whole. It allows us to see the value and meaning of our own contribution. Instead of watching helplessly as each successive crisis crashes over the world, whipped to a frenzy by the media, we can share

God's view of events and take counsel with him. He has given us this world to explore, care for and enjoy. He has given us each other to belong together in families, friendships, communities and nations. He hasn't made us just to be reduced to a number on a bank account or a line on a print-out. Rather we take our place among his children—responsible stewards of his creation, active agents for peace, and tireless messengers of his love.

Prayer helps us to make sense of the world and to see the value and meaning of our own contribution

IS ANYBODY THERE?

For some people prayer seems to be the easiest thing in the world. Their prayer is thoughtful and fluent—and it seems they can turn it on and off like a tap!

But for most of us prayer is often quite hard and sometimes impossible. We can't help wondering whether God is really interested in the everyday doings of our little lives. We can't help wondering whether he's there at all, or whether we're simply wasting our time. Our thoughts disappear into an open sky, or bounce back at us from the ceiling.

All of us who pray have this experience. There are times—perhaps even long periods of time—when we seem to be waiting for God. All we can say of him is that he doesn't seem to be around. But as we continue to be available to him, we become aware that he is in fact all around us—and within us. He is everywhere and very close.

And then we have to smile with recognition, and wonder afresh at

Any which way

There must be as many ways of praying as there are people to pray.

There is certainly no single, sure-fire method of prayer which is guaranteed to work for every person every time. As with any friendship, we will thrive on variety in our life with God. Do lovers or close friends meet only in the same place at the same time each day to talk about the same things? Surely not!

So variety is the spice of prayer.

• Sometimes we may pray 'off the top' as the things we want to talk to God about come naturally to our lips.

• Sometimes we may want to distil our prayers in carefully chosen words and write them down.

• Sometimes we may use the prayers that others have written, or we may turn our Bible study into prayer, allowing the psalms or the teachings of Jesus or the apostle Paul to nourish and inform our communication with God.

• We may use a form of prayer set out in a prayer book, or settle into silence, or float into 'tongues' (see page 61). We may even burst into song!

As to posture, we may sit or kneel, walk or run—or dance.

Whatever we do, we have this one aim: to express the love and longing of our hearts towards God, and to be open to his purpose in our lives.

be predicted, demanded or explained. It will be unique.

But when we are frustrated by the apparent 'absence' of God, have we ever stopped to consider that he has waited an eternity for us? There must be many times every day when we would hear God's approach if we would only listen. But instead we give him the call-back-on-busy signal, assure him of our best attention at a later date, and think no more about him.

For most of us, whatever our age or experience, prayer is sometimes hard. But as we continue to be open to God, we become aware of his presence and know he is listening

our own spiritual blindness and lack of faith. We've fallen into the oldest trap of all, which is to think that God must come running because we've finally decided to give him a few minutes of our attention. We thought we could oblige him to meet with us, and that we would dictate the terms of friendship. How wrong we were! We can no more force a relationship with the Living God than we can with anyone else.

As we open our hearts to God, he'll surely make himself known to us in his own way and in his own time. The particular way in which he deals with each of us can never

Praying for God's grace

May God our Father and the Lord Jesus Christ give you grace and peace.

I thank my God for you every time I think of you; and every time I pray for you all, I pray with joy because of the way you have helped me in the work of the gospel from the very first day until now. And so I am sure that God, who began this good work in you, will carry it on until it is finished on the Day of Christ Jesus . .

I pray that your love will keep on growing more and more, together with true knowledge and perfect judgment, so that you will be able to choose what is best. Then you will be free from all impurity and blame on the Day of Christ. Your lives will be filled with the truly good qualities which only Jesus Christ can produce, for the glory and praise of God.

PAUL'S PRAYER FOR THE PHILIPPIANS

Evere since I heard of your faith in the Lord Jesus and your love for all God's people, I have not stopped giving thanks to God for you. I remember you in my prayers and ask the God of our Lord Jesus Christ, the glorious Father, to give you the Spirit, who will make you wise and reveal God to you, so that you will know him. I ask that your minds may be opened to see his light, so that you will know what is the hope to which he has called you, how rich are the wonderful blessings he promises to his people, and how very great is his power at work in us who believe.

PAUL'S PRAYER FOR THE EPHESIANS

DISCOVERING
JESUS

Before we can discover prayer, we must discover
Jesus. When Jesus walked this earth, he really
prayed. And he taught others to pray; not by
running seminars but by being caught in the act.
His whole life was a prayer.

THE LIVING WAY

In the Gospels, there are seventeen recorded instances of Jesus praying. They're scattered throughout the account of his public ministry, from the day he was baptized to the moment he died.

Maybe the disciples got used to waking up to find Jesus' bed already empty. But in the early days it was a surprise. Mark's Gospel records:

Very early the next morning, long before daylight, Jesus got up and left the house. He went out of the town to a lonely place, where he prayed. But Simon and his companions went out searching for him ...

As weeks and months went by, they continued to wonder at this strange phenomenon—a person who actually enjoyed praying! Jesus' life seemed to flow in and out of prayer in such a way that you couldn't even see the join. In the end, the curiosity of the disciples got the better of them. Luke's Gospel tells us:

One day Jesus was praying in a certain place. When he had finished, one of his disciples said to him, "Lord, teach us to pray ...'

And so Jesus taught them the prayer we know as the Lord's Prayer—God-centred, realistic, heartfelt and short (see page 40). He followed it with a cluster of sparkling word pictures:

God loves to hear from us.

He will gladly respond to our approach. He's not like a sleepy neighbour we're trying to coax from bed in the middle of the night.

God is real.

He is there. He's not a practical joker who invites us to ask for something he'll never give us, or sets us to look for something we'll never find. Nor does he urge us to knock at a door which can never open.

He is like a father who loves to give good things to his children. His best gift of all is his Holy Spirit. And all we have to do is ask.

The only barriers between us and God are the ones we create. God has promised that the door is always open

WHEN DID JESUS PRAY?

We've already seen that prayer was part of Jesus' life.

- At each major milestone in his ministry we find him at prayer.

- It was while he was praying after his baptism that the Holy Spirit settled on him like a dove, and the voice of God the Father announced that Jesus was indeed his 'own dear Son'.

- He prayed all night before choosing his inner circle of twelve disciples.

- Jesus was obviously much in prayer after Peter had recognized him as the Messiah and there was a strong ground swell of opinion that he should proclaim himself King of the Jews. But Jesus knew full well that his road to glory must take him through suffering and death.

- On the night of his arrest he prayed most movingly for his disciples and those who would become his followers in all the ages to come. Later, in the dark groves of the Garden of Gethsemane, we see the sweat pouring off him as he wrestles with the Father's purpose and his destiny on the cross.

In these events we see a man—a perfect man—whose prayers were real. This may surprise us. Maybe

A friend at midnight

Jesus said to his disciples,

Suppose one of you should go to a friend's house at midnight and say to him, 'Friend, let me borrow three loaves of bread. A friend of mine who is on a long journey has just come to my house, and I haven't got any food for him!' And suppose your friend should answer from inside, 'Don't bother me! The door is already locked, and my children and I are in bed. I can't get up and give you anything.'

Well, what then? I tell you that even if he will not get up and give you the bread because you are his friend, yet he will get up and give you everything you need because you are not ashamed to keep on asking.

And so I say to you: Ask, and you will receive; seek, and you will find; knock, and the door will be opened to you. For everyone who asks will receive, and he who seeks will find, and the door will be opened to anyone who knocks.

Would any of you who are fathers give your son a snake when he asks for a fish? Or would you give him a scorpion when he asks for an egg? Bad as you are, you know how to give good things to your children. How much more, then, will the Father in heaven give the Holy Spirit to those who ask him!

THE GOSPEL OF LUKE

31

we assume that because Jesus was the Son of God, he had no need of prayer—he would instinctively know what God expected of him, and happily get on and do it. Instead we see a man for whom prayer was a lifeline. His prayer was indispensable if God's Spirit was to work within him and if he was to fulfil his mission to lay down his life for the sins of humankind.

How did Jesus manage to align himself totally with the Father's will? How did he handle criticism and conflict so superbly well? How did his teaching come to be the clearest and deepest that the world has seen? How could he harness and focus the healing power of God to mend broken lives? All these astonishing achievements have

their roots in his life of prayer.

And when we watch in horror as Jesus is so brutally hung up to die, we hear him praying still. Instead of a torrent of rage and self-pity, we hear him praying for his torturers —his cry that God will forgive them almost drowned by the sound of the nails being driven home.

In death as in life, Jesus was a man of prayer.

The Sovereign Lord has taught me what to say, so that I can strengthen the weary. Every morning he makes me eager to hear what he is going to teach me.

THE BOOK OF ISAIAH

We need to follow Jesus' example and put some space between ourselves and the busy world around us so that we can spend time alone with God

HOW DID JESUS PRAY?

We have already said that prayer isn't a method, but rather a way of life. However, some of the details of Jesus' life give us vital pointers to effective prayer.

Jesus made space

When Jesus wanted to pray, he put some distance, however small, between himself and his everyday distractions. In a culture that had turned prayer into a spectator sport—with religious superstars intoning record-breaking prayers on every street corner—Jesus hid away. In the pressure of an incredibly busy life, with people's expectations of him mounting to fever pitch, he would frequently and regularly take time to pray.

We know from the Gospels that he made time and space for prayer by climbing mountains or by walking the desert. We know that sometimes he got up early to spend time with his heavenly Father. On occasions he would give a whole night to prayer. Always we see him favouring the lonely places and the quiet times.

But far from marking Jesus out as a recluse, we see that such withdrawal formed a reservoir of spiritual refreshment. In prayer he basked in the Father's love. He asked for, and received, the wisdom and insight he needed. He recharged his spiritual batteries, returning to his task with renewed mental alertness and physical vigour.

In prayer Jesus was not just a container to catch God's blessing, but a channel through which healing power could flow to others. He found the balance between preaching God's love and declaring God's anger. He discerned the truth about himself—that he must plumb the very depths of suffering and only then would the Father raise him to glory.

Jesus harnessed emotion

Jesus was fully human, and he experienced the full range of human emotions. We see him ecstatic when God's work is going well. At other times we detect clear signs of frustration, exasperation and fatigue. There are times when he is downright angry—and eloquent with it. And once or twice he weeps unashamedly—at the tomb of his friend Lazarus, or when he perceives the appalling tragedy which will befall his beloved Jerusalem.

But instead of following his deep sighs of frustration or grief with a helpless shrug, Jesus channelled his feelings into prayer. Instead of allowing anger and frustration to

When we pray, the simpler our prayers are the better; the plainest, humblest language which expresses our meaning is the best.

C.H. SPURGEON

33

lock him into a prison of depression, Jesus presented his agony of soul to his heavenly Father.

There is a clue here for us. To 'let things out' to God, to tell him how it is for us—even to let him have our rage and defiance in no uncertain terms.

Jesus never used prayer to defy God the Father or threaten disobedience. But he clearly ploughed his fear and perplexity into prayer on many occasions— most importantly in Gethsemane, as Luke's Gospel records:

'Father, if you will, take this cup of suffering away from me. Not my will, however, but your will be done ...' In great anguish he prayed even more fervently; his sweat was like drops of blood falling to the ground.

And again on the cross:

Jesus cried out in a loud voice, 'Father! In your hands I place my spirit!' He said this and died.

Jesus was open to God

When Jesus prayed he was open to the guidance of God his Father. Near the end of the first chapter of Mark's Gospel, we read about Jesus actually changing the way he did things as a result of his prayer time. Up until then he had kept his base in the lakeside town of Capernaum, with people coming from far and wide in search of healing. But now he resolved to take to the road himself: 'We must go on to the other villages round here. I have to preach in them also, because that is why I came.'

It was evidently through prayer that Jesus realized both his job definition ('to seek and to save the lost'), and his style of ministry ('the Son of Man came not to be served but to serve and to give his life').

But this clarity of insight was only gained after a hard fight to resist other ways of going about his work. Right at the beginning of his public life, we read of Satan bombarding Jesus with 'helpful' ideas. If he was God's Son, why didn't he help himself and others by turning stone to bread? Why not do a deal with Satan and rule the world? Why not capture public attention by throwing himself from the summit of the temple?

In each instance (and who knows, there may have been many more), Jesus parried the temptations by quoting from the Old Testament. In this way we find him discovering God's mind—the kind of Messiah that God the Father wants his Son to be. Indeed, the kind of Messiah Jesus *must* be if he is to avoid the traps of self-centredness, status-seeking and sensationalism.

Late on in his ministry, some Greeks approached Jesus. No doubt they wanted to invite this outstanding teacher and wonder-worker to return with them to Greece and so embark on a whole new area of work. And how tempting that must have been for Jesus, for whom death was a few days away. His reply to them is as deep as it is moving, as the account in John's Gospel tells us:

Wrestling Jacob

There is a moving example in the pages of the Old Testament of a man thrashing out his personal identity in prayer. Jacob, Abraham's grandson, was a liar and a cheat. As a young man he had to flee from home to escape the wrath of his twin brother Esau.

The Bible tells how he had a remarkable dream when he was friendless and on the run:

He saw a stairway reaching from earth to heaven, with angels going up and coming down on it. And there was the Lord standing beside him. 'I am the Lord, the God of Abraham and Isaac,' he said. 'I will give to you and to your descendants this land on which you are lying. They will be as numerous as the specks of dust on the earth . . . Remember, I will be with you and protect you wherever you go.'

So Jacob discovered not only that God is for real, but that the Living God knew *him*—knew all about him, and had plans for his life. Jacob never forgot his vision of God that night.

Many years later, when God had blessed him with a large family and much wealth, Jacob was panicked by the news that he was about to meet Esau again. There followed the worst night of his life—or was it the best?

A man came and wrestled with him until just before daybreak. When the man saw that he was not winning the struggle, he struck Jacob on the hip, and it was thrown out of joint. The man said, 'Let me go; daylight is coming.'

'I won't, unless you bless me,' Jacob answered.

'What is your name?' the man asked.

'Jacob,' he answered.

The man said, 'Your name will no longer be Jacob. You have struggled with God and with men, and you have won; so your name will be Israel.' Jacob said, 'Now tell me your name.' But he answered, 'Why do you want to know my name?' Then he blessed Jacob. Jacob said, 'I have seen God face to face, and I am
still alive;' so he named the place Peniel. The sun rose as Jacob was leaving Peniel, and he was limping because of his hip.

All that Jacob was, and all that he had achieved, hung in the balance. Could his flawed character and dubious motives survive this trial of strength with God?

Jacob lived to tell the tale—and was wonderfully reconciled with Esau. But he was a changed man. He had a new name—'Israel' (which means, 'He struggles with God'). He had a new depth of understanding of himself. And to the end of his days he walked with a limp.

Now my heart is troubled—and what shall I say? Shall I say, 'Father, do not let this hour come upon me'? But this is why I came—so that I might go through this hour of suffering. Father, bring glory to your name!'

Here we see the beginning, middle and end of Jesus' prayer: 'Father, glorify your name!' When Jesus said this he summarized every prayer he had ever prayed, and captured the meaning and method of his whole life.

For Jesus, prayer was never a way of asking God the Father to endorse his own decisions. Rather it was a constant aligning of his life and work to the mind, will and character of God. And so he could say:

I am telling you the truth: the Son can do nothing on his own; he does only what he sees his Father doing. What the Father does, the Son also does.

Expecting answers

We should cultivate the habit of expecting answers to our prayers. We should do like the merchant who sends his ships to sea. We should not be satisfied unless we see some return.

J.C. RYLE

Try not to let the prayers you make to the Lord be words of mere politeness.

TERESA OF AVILA

Prayers in the Old Testament

Arguing with God

Abraham approached the Lord and asked, 'Are you really going to destroy the innocent with the guilty? If there are fifty innocent people in the city, will you destroy the whole city? Won't you spare it in order to save the fifty? Surely you won't kill the innocent with the guilty. That's impossible! You can't do that. If you did, the innocent would be punished along with the guilty. That is impossible. The judge of all the earth has to act justly.'

ABRAHAM'S PRAYER FOR SODOM TO BE SPARED, IN GENESIS

Driving a bargain

Jacob made a vow to the Lord: 'If you will be with me and protect me on the journey I am making and give me food and clothing, and if I return safely to my father's home, then you will be my God. This memorial stone which I have set up will be the place where you are worshipped, and I will give you a tenth of everything you give me.'

JACOB'S PRAYER AT BETHEL, IN GENESIS

Praying for wisdom

That night God appeared to Solomon and asked, 'What would you like me to give you?'

Solomon answered, 'You always showed great love for my father David, and now you have let me succeed him as king. O Lord God, fulfil the promise you made to my father. You have made me king over a people who are so many that they cannot be counted, so give me the wisdom and knowledge I need to rule over them. Otherwise, how would I ever be able to rule this great people of yours?'

God replied to Solomon, 'You have made the right choice. Instead of asking for wealth or treasure or fame or the death of your enemies or even for long life for your-self, you have asked for wisdom and knowledge so that you can rule my people, over whom I have made you king. I will give you wisdom and know-ledge. And in addition, I will give you more wealth, treasure, and fame than any king has ever had before or will ever have again.'

SOLOMON'S PRAYER ON BECOMING KING

Praying for a nation

Daniel prayed, 'Lord God, you are great, and we honour you. You are faithful to your covenant and show constant love to those who love you and do what you command.

'We have sinned, we have been evil, we have done wrong. We have rejected what you commanded us to do and have turned away from what you showed us was right . . .

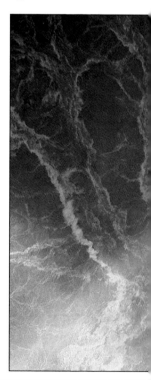

'Our kings, our rulers, and our ancestors have acted shamefully and sinned against you, Lord. You are merciful and forgiving, although we have rebelled against you...

'Listen to us, O God; look at us, and see the trouble we are in and the suffering of the city that bears your name. We are praying to you because you are merciful, not because we have done right. Lord, hear us. Lord, forgive us. Lord, listen to us, and act! In order that everyone will know that you are God, do not delay! This city and these people are yours.'

THE BOOK OF DANIEL

Promising to give

There in front of the whole assembly King David praised the Lord. He said, 'Lord God of our ancestor Jacob, may you be praised for ever and ever! You are great and powerful, glorious, splendid, and majestic. Everything in heaven and earth is yours, and you are king, supreme ruler over all. All riches and wealth come from you; you rule everything by your strength and power; and you are able to make anyone great and strong. Now, our God, we give you thanks, and we praise your glorious name.

Yet my people and I cannot really give you anything, because everything is a gift from you, and we have only given back what is yours already.'

DAVID'S PRAYER WHEN HE AND THE WHOLE NATION PRESENTED THEIR GIFTS FOR THE BUILDING OF THE TEMPLE

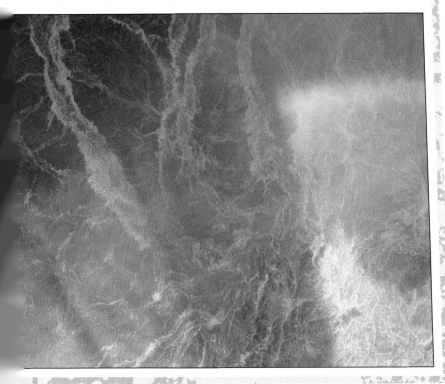

A STANDARD OF PRAYING

When the disciples asked Jesus to teach them to pray, he responded with a model prayer—beautiful, balanced and brief. It has come to be known as the Lord's Prayer, and it has been prayed in every age and in many languages. Here is a modern rendering taken from the Gospel of Luke:

Father: May your holy name be honoured;
may your Kingdom come.
Give us day by day the food we need.
Forgive us our sins,
for we forgive everyone who does wrong.
And do not bring us to hard testing.

What does this prayer teach us about our own praying?

The Lord's Prayer — God-centred, realistic, heartfelt and short — is a model prayer for us to follow

We begin with God

Jesus reminds us who we are talking to. We're coming to Almighty God who is also our Father. We aren't phoning through a big order to a department store which sells everything. Nor are we practising some weird and wonderful thought-process guaranteed to release psychic powers. We're coming simply, humbly, into the presence of our Creator, having received the invitation to do so from Jesus himself.

It's good to remember that God is 'our Father'. We belong to a great trans-national, cross-cultural family, some of whom have already died, and some of whom are yet to be born. Wherever we are around the world, and at whatever point in time we live, we own God as our Father and Jesus as our Lord. So when we pray this prayer, we're sharing with our Christian brothers and sisters, across every division of colour and class, of politics and economics, of time and eternity.

We say 'yes' to God

Not only do we begin with God, we also ask that all he wants to do in our lives and in our world may come about. We ask that men and women everywhere may realize who God is and humble themselves before him.

5

DISCOVERING OURSELVES

When we put God first in our lives, start to blurt out our thanks to him for his goodness and come clean with him about our problems; then we're not just about to discover prayer—we're already praying.

We ask that God's kingdom may come

The kingdom of God exists wherever God is king. It isn't located on a map, nor do we enter it by holding a passport! The exciting truth is that God is already king of millions of lives. He is already acknowledged as Lord in a vast number of situations. We see the effects of his rule when hate is disarmed by love, when bitterness is dissolved by forgiveness, when disease is overwhelmed by health, and when war is defeated by peace.

But we must remember that God is a father and not a dictator. For this reason his kingdom can only come when individual people invite him into their lives and submit themselves to the changes he wants to make.

This phrase, 'May your kingdom come', more than any other in the Lord's Prayer, has a tendency to rebound on the user. If we really want God's kingdom to come, then we must open ourselves and our circumstances to God, whatever the cost.

And if we're looking for the kind of changes in the world that only God can make, we may find that he promptly enlists us in his service! We may find ourselves doing anything from bathing an invalid to mailing a cheque for famine relief. We may even find that we are called to throw our own life into a particular situation as the only fitting contribution we can make to God's work there.

We bring our needs to God

In the second half of the Lord's Prayer we ask God to meet our basic human needs. We ask him for enough to live on, for forgiveness, and for protection.

'Give us day by day the food we need'

This has a strong echo of the days when the Israelites were supplied with manna in the desert. Every day they had 'enough', and the Lord's Prayer asks that we may have the same experience of God's faithful provision each day as it comes. In the Sermon on the Mount, Jesus had this to say:

Do not start worrying: 'Where will my food come from? or my drink? or my clothes?' (These are the things the pagans are always concerned about.) Your Father in heaven knows that you need all these things. Instead, be concerned above everything else with the Kingdom of God and with what he requires of you, and he will provide you with all these other things.

In an age when many people are run ragged by their desire for money and possessions, this is a wonderful promise from Jesus. All the same, we should notice that it is everything we *need* that God will provide, and not everything we want.

'Forgive us our sins, for we forgive everyone who does us wrong.'

This reminds us that our standard of living is more than a roof over our head, food on the table and a

We have to make peace with anyone against whom we are harbouring anger or resentment. When we forgive others we can receive God's forgiveness

shirt on our back. Our well-being is intimately tied up with personal relationships—within ourselves, between each other and between ourselves and God.

Our recurring need here is for forgiveness. We hurt people by our self-centredness, our anger and our prejudice. We hurt God by going our own way in defiance of his loving law, wilfully defiling all that he intended life in this world to be.

So we ask for forgiveness. We feel the need and we say the words. But it's no easy matter for God to forgive us. It cost him the life of his only son to show the reality and consequence of sin. As he died on the cross, Jesus took on himself the results of all our sin. This is the only way by which we can be forgiven and restored to spiritual life. This is the Christian good news: that new life with God— something we can never earn and certainly don't deserve—is his free

gift to us through the death of Jesus. Our sins are not only forgiven but forgotten, and if we mention them to God again he'll wonder what we're talking about.

But as we ask God to forgive us, we must check if there is anyone who in turn needs our forgiveness. How do we feel about our worst enemy? Is there any member of the family, or anybody at work, against whom we're nursing anger, bitterness or resentment? Only as we forgive others can we enter fully into the wonderful experience of God's forgiveness of us.

Sometimes we may have to stop our praying of the Lord's Prayer at this point and take Jesus' advice in the Sermon on the Mount:

If you are about to offer your gift to God at the altar and there you remember that your brother has something against you, leave your gift there in front of the altar, go at once and make peace with your brother,

and then come back and offer your gift to God.

This is not just a nice idea. It's a condition for our own forgiveness. Elsewhere Jesus warns that if we don't forgive, then we in turn shall not be forgiven. This teaching alone, if we take it seriously, will completely change our lives.

'And do not bring us to hard testing.'

Sometimes this is translated, 'Lead us not into temptation,' and we may well wonder when, why and how God could possibly want us to be tempted. And we would be right—he doesn't. The letter from James tells us where temptations to do evil come from:

A person is tempted when he is drawn away and trapped by his own evil desire. Then his evil desire conceives and gives birth to sin; and sin, when it is full-grown, gives birth to death.

But while God will never lure us into evil, he will sometimes allow us to be tested. Just as we will put ourselves through all kinds of discomfort to get fit or lose weight, so God will allow pressure on us in order to strengthen our faith or increase our insight.

In the face of this testing, Jesus includes a very human plea that God won't go over the top in his efforts to refine us. It is encouraging to hear Jesus say this, because he was tempted over a longer period and with greater intensity than we'll ever know. Enticed by Satan, or daunted by God, we often give in

at a very early stage. Our Christian integrity disintegrates and we snatch at hypocrisy to cover our shame. But while we often capitulate, Jesus never did so. Not once. The writer to the Hebrews tells us that Jesus was 'tempted in every way that we are, but did not sin'. And when Jesus invited his toughest critics to bring charges against him, they were reduced to silence.

The Lord's Prayer recognizes that temptation is an integral part of our daily life. We'll never lose it, so we must learn to use it. James writes: 'Consider yourselves fortunate when all kinds of trials come your way, for you know that when your faith succeeds in facing such trials, the result is the ability to endure.'

If we can use the force of temptations to push us closer to the Lord, rather than sweeping us away from him, then we'll be harnessing their power for our benefit.

Thou art our peace, O Lord.
From the thousand wearinesses
of our daily life, from the
disappointments, from nervous
and senseless haste, we turn to
thee and are at peace. The
clamour dies, we are alive in the
sunshine of thy presence. Even
so come, Lord Jesus, to this soul
of mine.

MARTHA'S PRAYER BOOK

TURN AGAIN

We've already seen that God is holy but we're sinful. The sinful nature in all of us sets us poles apart from God. He is all that is right, loving and pure. We are often wrong, selfish and unclean.

So whenever we come to God in prayer, we need to 'turn round'. This is what repentance means: not just saying sorry, but decisively changing direction—altering course to get on line with the will of God.

Sometimes we may feel we've been doing rather well. We've done someone a good turn, curbed a bad habit and smiled sweetly at someone who swore at us. All in all we've had a good day!

In fact what we mean by this is that we think we're better than some people we know. But when we hold up our lives and see them in the light of God's holiness, we can discern some nasty stains. The apostle John wrote in one of his letters, 'If we say that we have not sinned, we make God out to be a liar.' He explained it this way:

If we say that we have no sin, we deceive ourselves, and there is no truth in us. But if we confess our sins to God, he will keep his promise and do what is right: he will forgive us our sins and purify us from all our wrongdoing.

So long as we walk this earth we will be sinful. Sin is selfishness. It's in our system. It's part of our nature. And it isn't something we can ever grow out of, as the greatest saints know well. Paul wrote to the Romans:

I know that good does not live in me— that is, in my human nature. For even though the desire to do good is in me, I am not able to do it. I don't do the good I want to do; instead, I do the evil that I do not want to do ... It is the sin that lives in me.

And so, day by day, even hour by hour, we need to turn to God for cleansing.

According to John's Gospel, Jesus gave his disciples a picture of spiritual hygiene as well as of serving others when he washed their feet. Simon Peter was shocked and embarrassed when Jesus knelt before him with a bowl and towel and set about the slave's work of foot-washing:

Peter declared, 'Never at any time will you wash my feet!'

'If I do not wash your feet,' Jesus answered, 'you will no longer be my disciple.'

Simon Peter answered, 'Lord, do not wash only my feet, then! Wash my hands and head, too!'

According to Jewish custom, all the disciples would have bathed before going out for the evening meal. But as they made their way through the streets, their feet would have got dirty again—perhaps only picking up dust, or maybe treading in something worse! And so, on arrival at the house, they would be

met by a slave with a bowl of water and a towel.

This is a clear picture of what happens to us. When we turn to God through Jesus, our sinfulness is forgiven and we are welcomed into God's family. But because we continue to live in this world, we can't help but pick up the world's dirt. It may seem nothing much, but it's still something that only Jesus can deal with. Of course, like Peter, we may feel embarrassed, but we must in the end allow Jesus to wash us.

We can quietly tell God about our sins and ask his forgiveness through Jesus. Sometimes it helps to talk it through with someone we can trust. In his letter James wrote: 'Confess your sins to one another and pray for one another, so that you will be healed.'

This is actually advice as to how to pray for healing of physical illness, but it holds for spiritual disease as well. The person we choose to talk to should be a mature Christian—someone we can trust not to go gossiping about us, and who we know will pray for us. You may settle into a regular pattern of meeting each week or each month to help each other. And don't feel embarrassed to ask for help. From popes to peasants (and that includes parsons!), we all need a trusted Christian friend to show us the acceptance, forgiveness, cleansing and love of Jesus.

And what a relief! To realize that Jesus knows the worst about us— that he will set to, muck us out and still love us—this is better than a month in the Bahamas. After struggling along with our burden of failure and guilt, we at last find ourselves back home with God— showered, fed, refreshed and relaxed. And no one is happier about this than God himself. Jesus captures it all in the parable of the lost son, found in the Gospel of Luke:

The son was still a long way from home when his father saw him; his heart was filled with pity, and he ran, threw his arms round his son, and kissed him.

We can't be passive with God. We have to put energy into developing our relationship with him. If faith is to grow, we have to work at it

'Father,' the son said, 'I have sinned against God and against you. I am no longer fit to be called your son.'

But the father called his servants. 'Hurry!' he said. 'Bring the best robe and put it on him. Put a ring on his finger and shoes on his feet. Then go and get the prize calf and kill it, and let us celebrate with a feast! For this son of mine was dead, but now he is alive; he was lost, but now he has been found.' And so the feasting began.

THE ACTIVE INGREDIENT

What's the difference between a prayer which is just a string of empty words and prayer which is real? Faith. Faith is the active ingredient that delights God more than anything else.

What kind of faith?

The faith to put God first

We tell God that he's the most important person in our lives. We can never praise and thank him enough for all he means to us and all he's done for us. Only our best is good enough for him, and we ask that he'll accept the offering of our whole selves—and use us for his glory.

The faith to make a move

In an English comic opera, *The Pirates of Penzance*, the policemen march round the stage singing heroically, 'We go! We go!' as they prepare to tackle the pirates. But as the marching and singing continues, the ladies looking on are obliged to observe, 'But you *don't* go!'

How many Christians, both individually and as congregations, live in this state of energetic paralysis? When faith is present, there are fewer fanfares but more quiet effective action. In the Bible we find men and women who were prepared to live out their faith. In

47

spite of all the laughter, hostility or indifference that public opinion heaped upon them, they put God first and acted accordingly.

Noah built a giant boat hundreds of miles from the sea—in a part of the world that had never known rain, never mind flooding. As a result of his faith, he and his family, together with many species of animals, were able to survive the disaster of God's judgment.

Just as remarkably, an elderly man by the name of Abraham renounced the comforts of city life and became a wandering herdsman, for no other reason than that he felt God calling him to do so. Indeed, Abraham's experience was so revolutionary that the Bible describes him as 'the father of the faithful'.

The great Baptist missionary, William Carey, urged Christians to 'expect great things from God; attempt great things for God'. When we live this way, our priorities and reactions may appear decidedly odd, but in fact they make sense when it is seen that we are living and moving in God's magnetic field.

The faith that God will win

At the heart of our faith is the assurance of God's victory: his triumph over the sin within us, the problems around us, and death ahead of us.

In the Old Testament there are many instances of God rescuing people against all the odds. Young Joseph, who was thrown into a pit by his brothers and then sold as a slave, survived to become prime minister of Egypt. He gave all the glory to God. A thousand years later, a Jewish official in Babylon was sentenced to be torn apart by lions, and his colleagues were to be burned alive. Yet all four emerged from their ordeals unscathed, and the emperor who had inflicted such punishments had to admit that only the Living God could have delivered them.

In the New Testament even these epic adventures are put in the shade by the triumphant resurrection of Jesus of Nazareth after his death by crucifixion. For all Christians this is the key demonstration of God's power to save those who put their trust in him. We have an Easter faith. We believe in a God who brings his people out of darkness into light, out of slavery into freedom, and out of spiritual death into spiritual life.

The real me

As long as we ourselves are real, as long as we are truly ourselves, God can be present and can do something with us. But the moment we try to be what we are not, there is nothing left to say or have; we become a fictitious personality, an unreal presence, and this unreal presence cannot be approached by God.

ARCHBISHOP ANTHONY OF SOUROZH

48

The Christian life isn't a cure-all for every problem, imperfection and disease. But trusting in a God who has triumphed over these things provides hope for us in even the most unpromising situations

The faith that hangs in there

And yet, having said that, the Christian life is clearly not a triumphant procession along a primrose path. Faith in God is by no means a cure-all for every disease. It doesn't mend deformed babies or divert terrorist bullets or steer runaway buses. If it did, there would surely be more takers!

For some, the life of faith is a rocky, uphill and almost invisible path through suffering. Because of illness, misfortune or persecution, they have no great story of deliverance to tell.

And there are people like this in the Bible too. One of the oldest stories of all is that of Job, who lost both his children and his property in a series of disasters and was himself afflicted with a repulsive disease. Much later, we read of Jesus' own cousin, John the Baptist, whose courageous witness and bold preaching were cut short when he was executed during a drunken party at the whim of a young woman and her mother.

And if we doubt that such suffering and tragedy are in fact allowed by God, then we must look again at what happened to Jesus.

Nitty-gritty

The Bible is packed with sinners!

On page after page we see the effects of sin, even in the lives of the greatest men and women of faith.

We meet the first pair of brothers, and watch in horror as one kills the other because of jealousy. To this very day, most murders are committed within the family.

Joseph's pride and self-centredness (encouraged by his father's misguided favouritism) led to his brothers attacking him and selling him as a slave.

King Saul couldn't live with David's popularity and repeatedly tried to murder him.

David, once he'd become king, was so infatuated with the wife of one of his soldiers that he arranged for the man to be 'accidentally' killed in battle.

Among the disciples of Jesus, we hear frequent bickering and quarrelling about which of them is most important.

As Jesus is being crucified, we see law-abiding, deeply religious citizens coming to vent their spleen on him. Governor Pilate knew full well that the real reason for Jesus' arrest had been jealousy.

And in the gifted, gutsy young church at Corinth, we find rampant party spirit. People taking sides and forming personality cults in an attempt to prove them-selves right and everyone else wrong.

So jealousy and envy are part of our lives. They do damage at home, at the office, on the shop floor, in our classes and teams—and at church.

In the face of this insiduous evil, our secret weapon is forgiveness. When there's a flare-up at home or at work, we need to be the first to apologize and make amends. This doesn't mean running round everyone and becoming a pain in the neck with the intensity of our apologies. Rather, we must so enjoy and appreciate God's forgiveness of us that we have a reservoir of love to share.

Jesus was strong on forgiveness, as we see in Matthew's Gospel:

Do not take revenge on someone who wrongs you. If anyone slaps you on the right cheek, let him slap your left cheek too. And if someone takes you to court to sue you for your shirt, let him have your coat as well. And if one of the occupation troops forces you to carry his pack one kilometre, carry it two kilometres. When someone asks you for something, give it to him; when someone wants to borrow something, lend it to him.

You have heard that it was said, 'Love your friends, hate your enemies.' But now I tell you: love your enemies and pray for those who persecute you, so that you may become the sons of your Father in heaven.

And when Peter thinks he's finally got the message, Jesus still has a surprise in store.

Peter came to Jesus and asked, 'Lord, if my brother keeps on sinning against me, how many times do I have to forgive him? Seven times?'

'No, not seven times,' answered Jesus, 'but seventy times seven.'

During the course of his short life, and especially during his last hours, he endured every kind of affliction known to humanity, from betrayal by a close friend and miscarriage of justice to extreme forms of physical and mental abuse, exposure, defilement, torture and death.

More than anything else, the horror of what happened at the cross shows us that God's deliverance is for those who continue faithfully through suffering. We trust that God is with us in our darkness and pain, and that he'll bring us gloriously through—if not to a happy ending in this life, then to the healing and joyful fulfilment of his heaven. This is the faith that hangs in there against all the evidence and in every circumstance—a faith given to many millions of people around the world. It is a priceless treasure.

> Jesus does not patch things up. He renews. If you will ask him to go back with you to that dark spot in your life he will change its darkness into light. That was his purpose in coming to us. He delivered us from all sin.
>
> CORRIE TEN BOOM

ASKING FOR GOOD

In his teaching about prayer, Jesus was most insistent that we should ask God for good things. And not be afraid to go on asking! He tells two hilarious stories to illustrate persistent prayer.

One is about a man who pounds on his neighbour's door in the middle of the night because he wants to borrow some bread to feed an unexpected guest. In the end the neighbour clambers out of bed and throws the entire contents of his food cupboard out of the window in a desperate attempt to get rid of his friend before he wakes the children!

The other story is about a widow who is trying to get a fair ruling from a corrupt and slovenly judge. Although she's powerless to influence him by threats or bribes, eventually she wears him out with her nagging, and he gives her everything she wants.

Jesus doesn't tell these stories to illustrate God's reluctance to hear our prayers, but to highlight his *willingness* to answer our requests. If a sleepy neighbour or a reluctant judge will give in in the end, how much more quickly will our alert, loving and generous God respond to our cries?

All the same, there are some conditions we need to fulfil. For a start, what did Jesus pray about?

He prayed above all for people

During the Last Supper, John's Gospel tells us that Jesus prayed for his disciples—especially that God would keep them safe from the devil, and united in love:

Holy Father! Keep them safe by the power of your name, so that they may be one just as you and I are one. I do not ask you to take them out of the world, but I do ask you to keep them safe from the Evil One.

Later in the same prayer, Jesus prayed for us!

I pray also for those who believe in me ... I pray that they may all be one. Father! May they be in us, just as you are in me and I am in you. May they be one, so that the world will believe that you sent me.

We see that Jesus' overriding theme in his prayer for others was that they should be protected from evil and caught up, together with him, into God's love. In his Gospel, Luke gives us another glimpse of Jesus' prayer—an exchange with Simon Peter that same evening:

Simon, Simon! Listen! Satan has received permission to test all of you, to separate the good from the bad, as a farmer separates the wheat from the chaff. But I have prayed for you, Simon, that your faith will not fail.

Jesus is totally realistic about what lies ahead for Peter, and prays that Satan's attacks will in fact strengthen his faith, deepen his self-knowledge, and enable him to teach and encourage others in due course.

Jesus had time for children, and a very special blessing for them. We can pray for children with complete confidence that God loves them too

This is a prayer of the utmost maturity and courage, and we know from subsequent events that it was the making of Peter.

So far the prayers of Jesus put us completely in the shade. Is there no room for people like us who want to find someone nice to go out with, or long that our children should be safe crossing the road by them- selves, or crave relief from back-ache or some other nagging pain?

Yes, there is. Jesus taught his friends that God cared about the tiniest details of their lives—even

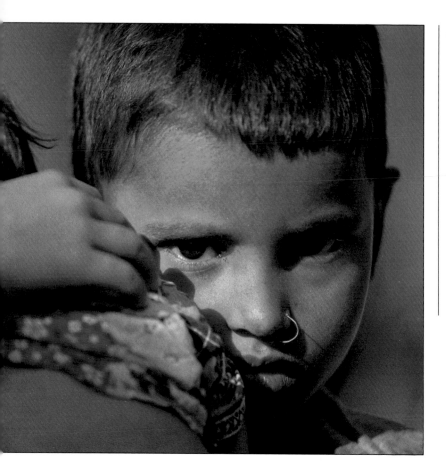

knowing the number of hairs on their heads! It is with this assurance that Peter writes in one of his letters, 'Cast all your anxiety on him, because he cares for you.'

Jesus prayed for children

In Mark's Gospel we hear of Jesus interrupting his conversation with adults to welcome and bless some children:

Some people brought children to Jesus for him to place his hands on them, but the disciples scolded the people.

When Jesus noticed this, he was angry and said to his disciples, 'Let the children come to me, and do not stop them, because the Kingdom of God belongs to such as these.'

And then Mark describes how Jesus took the children in his arms and blessed each one of them in turn. Jesus was delighted to see them, blessed them over and over again, and was reluctant to let them go.

Surely this incident encourages us to bring our loved ones to Jesus for his blessing.

And Jesus prayed for sick people

Luke tells us of a woman who wanted Jesus to help her, but was too shy and embarrassed to ask. Her problem was continuous period bleeding, and it had gone on for twelve years. All she dared do was edge up to Jesus in the crowd and tug at his coat—but she was cured. Jesus said,

'Someone touched me, for I knew it when power went out of me.'

The woman saw that she had been found out, so she came trembling and threw herself at Jesus' feet. There in front of everybody, she told him why she had touched him and how she had been healed at once. Jesus said to her, 'My daughter, your faith has made you well. Go in peace.'

This incident and many others like it encourage us to come to Jesus, no matter how deep-seated or secret our need. He won't be shocked, nor will he recoil in horror. Most of all, he won't send us away with orders to try harder in order to earn his love! Instead, he will give us his undivided attention. He may well grant us physical healing. Certainly he will commence our inner healing. And to everyone who comes to him he gives God's peace.

He prayed about people's ordinary decisions

And what about those who face major choices in their lives? Whether to marry, and if so, whom? What kind of training to go for, or which interests to cultivate? If this is our situation, and we are truly open to God's will for our lives, then Jesus has this to say in John's Gospel:

If you remain in me and my words remain in you, then you will ask for anything you wish, and you shall have it. My Father's glory is shown by your bearing much fruit; and in this way you become my disciples.

No agency names or numbers to call. Not even a computer printout which shortlists our options! All the same, if we commit our lives to live out this promise of Jesus, there will be no way we could be happier or more fulfilled.

If we love and trust God, then we can surely ask him to give us his best gifts. If we don't love or trust him, then why are we asking for anything at all?

Prayer at a distance

How little we realise the great importance of intercessory prayer. If at this moment you pray for someone, even though he is on the other side of the globe the Lord Jesus will touch him.

CORRIE TEN BOOM

ANYTHING WE ASK?

One of the most stunning promises Jesus ever made was on the theme of prayer:

If you remain in me and my words remain in you, then you will ask for anything you wish, and you shall have it.

It sounds like the ultimate open offer, doesn't it? We suddenly find ourselves in fairyland, where all our wishes will come true if only we tag on the magic name of Jesus!

But when we look closer at this teaching, we find there is much more to praying 'in Christ' than casting his name like a spell.

Jesus says that he's like a vine, and his followers are the branches. The two belong and grow together, and the central stem gives life to the branches so that they may bear fruit. As for God the Father, he's like the gardener who painstakingly cleans and tends the vine, pruning away the dead growth and encouraging the best possible yield of grapes.

So when Jesus says, 'If you remain in me and my words remain in you,' he's describing the conditions we need for right praying. Our lives need to be completely caught up in the life of Jesus, dependent on him for everything. This promise of Jesus has too often been ransacked by 'smash-and-grab' Christians in pursuit of good grades or attractive partners, who have neither the time nor the inclination to 'abide' in Christ and produce the fruit of his life in theirs.

This promise is really about God's desire to grow the life of Jesus in us, and this will involve us in costly commitment and painful pruning. If we throw in our lot with God, and allow our lives and attitudes to be changed and tuned, then we'll find ourselves wanting the same things that God wants.

We'll want his kingdom to spread. We'll want other people to get this good news about Jesus. We'll want God's power and love, his healing and peace, to be seen more clearly in our lives—not for our benefit, but for his glory.

Then of course we'll be able to ask for anything we wish, because we'll be wanting the very things that God wants.

Jesus used the vine and its branches to illustrate his relationship with his followers. Our lives need to be completely caught up in the life of Jesus

Jesus can understand

Fear not because your prayer is stammering, your words feeble, and your language poor. Jesus can understand you.

J.C. RYLE

Say 'Yes,' son. I need your 'yes' as I needed Mary's 'yes' to come to earth, for it is I who must do your work, it is I who must live in your family, it is I who must be in your neighbourhood, and not you . . . Give all to me, abandon all to me, I need your 'yes' to be united with you and to come down to earth, I need your 'yes' to continue saving the world!

MICHEL QUOIST

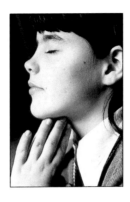

Lord, I thank you for your light
—I would never have known.
But, Lord, enough. I assure you I've understood.
I am nothing and you are all.

MICHEL QUOIST

Jesus is exactly the opposite of all that you are. If you are impure, he is pure; if you are unkind, he is gracious; if you are harsh and critical, he is love.

Never spend a moment trying to narrow the gap, but claim him as the opposite of everything you are by nature . . . He stands ready to reproduce his life in each one of us.

ALAN REDPATH

4

DISCOVERING
THE SPIRIT

We would have little hope of praying in Jesus' way
were it not for God's gift to us of the
Holy Spirit.

When the power
of the Holy Spirit
breaks into our
lives, our prayers
and worship will
be transformed

THE FRIEND IN NEED

On the night before his arrest and death, as John's Gospel records, Jesus promised his disciples that after he'd left them he would send 'the Helper' to them:

I am telling you the truth: it is better for you that I go away, because if I do not go, the Helper will not come to you. But if I do go away, then I will send him to you.

The Helper is none other than the Holy Spirit of God. He is the 'executive' branch of the Godhead. Wherever we see God at work, 'that's the Spirit!' And seven weeks after the crucifixion and resurrection of Jesus, the same Holy Spirit, the Spirit of Jesus, was sent to teach and empower the followers of Christ.

Yes! The Holy Spirit who was in Jesus of Nazareth also joins himself to his followers.

When the Holy Spirit was first given to the disciples, the Acts of the Apostles tells us that he sounded like a gale and looked like a brush fire:

Suddenly there was a noise from the sky which sounded like a strong wind blowing, and it filled the whole house where they were sitting. Then they saw what looked like tongues of fire which spread out and touched each person there. They were all filled with the Holy Spirit and began to talk in other languages, as the Spirit enabled them to speak.

The effect on the friends of Jesus was dramatic. They started to praise God and share the good news about Jesus in all the languages of the known world. The Helper was indeed coming to their assistance, transforming their communication with both God and people.

Soon the disciples were moving out of themselves, going beyond themselves, as they lived in the power of the Spirit. They showed signs of having the life of Jesus within them, and went about doing some of the things that Jesus had done.

The images of wind and fire linger in the mind as we read the story of the church in those early days. Although Jesus had spent his entire life in a remote corner of the Roman Empire, the story of his death and resurrection spread to Asia, Africa, Greece and Rome within a generation. The men who carried the burning news—notably Peter and Paul—were the first to admit that it was the presence and power of Jesus in their lives that enabled them to tackle this astonishing task.

The help of the Holy Spirit

We too need the help of the Holy Spirit, especially when we pray. The apostle Paul wrote to the church at Rome:

The Spirit makes you God's children, and by the Spirit's power we cry out to God, 'Father! my Father!' God's Spirit joins himself to our spirits to declare that we are God's children.

And then almost immediately comes a startling admission. The great apostle Paul himself admits that he is helpless when he tries to pray:

The Spirit comes to help us, weak as we are. For we do not know how we ought to pray; the Spirit himself pleads with God for us in groans that words cannot express. And God, who sees into our hearts, knows what the thought of the Spirit is; because the Spirit pleads with God on behalf of his people and in accordance with his will.

Here is one of the most important secrets of the life of prayer. We must call a halt to all 'do-it-yourself' efforts by which we try to pump up our prayers. Instead we must, in the old phrase, 'let go and let God'. Instead of struggling to know God's will, or groping for the right words,

we must ask the Holy Spirit to help us in our praying.

Because he is the Spirit of God, he knows the mind of God. Because he dwells within our own hearts, he can detect our deepest longings and interpret them to our heavenly Father. Because he is the Spirit of Jesus, he knows life on earth from the inside, and can plead our limitations and dilemmas with a passion that goes beyond words.

But best of all, because he is the Spirit of God, he can catch us up into the love of God. He can inspire our praises and ignite our prayers. With the Holy Spirit in our lives, we become living temples—mini worship-centres, alive with praise, committed to service and geared to mission.

Praying to be filled

I ask God from the wealth of his glory to give you power through his Spirit to be strong in your hearts through faith. I pray that you may have your roots and foundation in love, so that you, together with all God's people, may have the power to understand how broad and long, how high and deep, is Christ's love. Yes, may you come to know his love—although it can never be fully known—and so be completely filled with the very nature of God.

PAUL'S LETTER TO THE EPHESIANS

Speaking in tongues

'Speaking in tongues' is a particular form of prayer which helps many people commune with God from their spirit.

Sometimes our praying is hindered because we find it hard to put our deepest thoughts into words—and yet we don't want to lapse into silence either. And here the gift of tongues is an enormous help because we can simply 'babble' our love and longing to God, not worried by inadequate vocabulary or inaccurate grammar.

Although we read of Jesus 'filled with joy by the Holy Spirit', we're never told that he prayed in tongues, and we've no record of it in his teaching.

However, when the Holy Spirit was given to the disciples on the day of Pentecost, we read that they were 'all filled with the Holy Spirit and began to talk in other languages, as the Spirit enabled them to speak'.

This kind of tongues speaking was a rare gift indeed. It was a God-given miracle of communication whereby people from all over the world heard God praised and Jesus proclaimed in their native languages. In Bible terms, it was actually a reversal of the damage done when the tower of Babel fell. In that Old Testament story people had tried to set themselves up as the centre of the world by building a tower which would reach to heaven.

But God intervened and destroyed the project by mixing up their language so that they could no longer understand one another.

The vast majority of people who speak in tongues today are not speaking any known language. Nor are they using this gift in missionary work to communicate across a language barrier. Rather they are babbling to God, much as a toddler 'talks scribble' to its delighted parents.

The apostle Paul was very experienced in such prayer, and he wrote to the Christians at Corinth to say that, while the gift of tongues was uplifting and upbuilding for the individual, it was of little use in public without a parallel gift of interpretation:

The person who speaks in strange tongues must pray for the gift to explain what he says. For if I pray in this way, my spirit prays indeed, but my mind has no part in it. What should I do, then? I will pray with my spirit, but I will pray also with my mind; I will sing with my spirit, but I will sing also with my mind.

'Speaking in tongues' is undeniably a gift of the Holy Spirit. But, like all gifts, it can lead to squabbles. If we have this gift, let's remember that it is a gift and beware of concluding that we are a superior form of humanity.

If it is a gift we lack, then of course we can ask God if it is something he wants us to have. But don't assume that if you can't 'babble' you aren't really a Spirit-filled Christian. If Jesus is your Lord and you know that God is your Father, then the Holy Spirit is alive and well in your life. Paul told the Corinthians:

No one can confess 'Jesus is Lord' unless he is guided by the Holy Spirit.

61

God's greatness

O Lord, our Lord,
    your greatness is seen in all the world!
Your praise reaches up to the heavens;
    it is sung by children and babies.
You are safe and secure from all your
    enemies;
    you stop anyone who opposes you.

When I look at the sky, which you have
    made,
    at the moon and the stars, which you
      set in their places—
what is man, that you think of him;
    mere man, that you care for him?

Yet you made him inferior only to
    yourself;
    you crowned him with glory and
      honour.
You appointed him ruler over everything
    you made;
    you placed him over all creation:
    sheep and cattle, and the wild animals
      too;
    the birds and the fish
    and the creatures in the seas.

Lord, our Lord,
    your greatness is seen in all the world!

PSALM 8

WORSHIP

Worship is an affair of the heart.

We gather together to tell God he's the greatest and we love him. As God's people, it's the most important thing we do. Peter reminded the first-generation Christians he was writing to:

You are the chosen race, the King's priests, the holy nation, God's own people, chosen to proclaim the wonderful acts of God, who called you out of darkness into his own marvellous light.

When Christians meet together for worship, there should be a clear structure and order to the service. But within this structure there must be room for God to move. And we must come expecting to *be* moved!

Jesus once explained the true nature of worship to a woman he met at a well. She obviously thought that it was all to do with special times and places, and she knew there was rivalry between her people (the Samaritans) and the Jews, because they worshipped in different temples built on different mountains. But Jesus had this to say, as John's Gospel records:

The time is coming and is already here, when by the power of God's Spirit people will worship the Father as he really is, offering him the true worship that he wants. God is Spirit, and only by the power of his Spirit can people worship him as he really is.

So according to Jesus, true worship is not so much 'What do we do?' but 'For whom are we doing it?' Once we realize that we're meeting to have dealings with the Living God, then our standard of worship will improve by leaps and bounds.

One thing's for sure: we'll stop being bored.

And since worship is for God's benefit (literally telling him what he is worth), then we should stop judging church services by what we can get out of them. Our prime concern is to give God pleasure, and to accept and encourage our fellow-believers.

Worship comes naturally. We all do it. The only trouble is that most of the time we worship the wrong things.

We go mad about football teams, pop stars and cars. We take off our shoes in the hallowed presence of a new carpet. We stand in the rain for hours in the hope of catching a glimpse of royalty or a president. And as to money, we'll give our waking hours to earning it and still go to sleep wishing we had more.

But in his letter to the Christians at Rome, Paul says:

Offer yourselves as a living sacrifice to God, dedicated to his service and pleasing to him. This is the true worship that we should offer.

In other words, there's only one person worthy of our worship, and that's God. If we're seeking satisfaction and fulfilment anywhere else, then we're looking in the wrong place. Sport is terrific,

64

Let God do the lifting!

Sometimes we drag ourselves to worship knowing that we've very little to offer, and wondering why we bother at all.

But when we look in the Bible, we discover that worship doesn't have to spring from us at all. It's God who makes the move.

When the angels appeared to the Bethlehem shepherds to announce the birth of Jesus, it wasn't because the men were out in the fields holding a night of prayer. They were merely getting on with their work, and God was as far from their minds as usual. But when they received the news, they were transformed. They were filled with joy. And after they'd seen the baby for themselves, they could talk and sing of nothing else.

Wherever we look, the principle is the same. Simon Peter fell on his knees in front of Jesus and worshipped him, not because he thought he was an excellent carpenter, but because he'd seen the miraculous catch of fish. Again, it was God who made the move and then the person who responded in worship.

In the Old Testament, we find that Moses was an exiled prince who had spent forty years leading sheep round a desert, when one day God spoke to him at the burning bush.

Jacob was a runaway looking for a job when God spoke to him in his sleep.

Isaiah was day-dreaming politics with only half an eye on the temple worship, when God caught him up in a majestic vision of heaven.

So when we come to worship, our best attitude is to wait on God and expect him to make himself known.

Of course we want the direction of worship to be from us to God. But we can't begin from there. We can only begin with God's love and grace—and the direction of these is from God to us.

but it's only a game. Film stars and pop stars are fascinating, but they're only fellow human beings. They get acne and suffer migraine the same as the rest of us.

And money? Money is a great help and an exciting resource if we use it well. But if money is our master, then we're certainly living in misery.

Paul challenges us to break the mould of this world's standards and other people's expectations, and to let God do something completely new with our lives:

Do not conform yourselves to the standards of this world, but let God transform you inwardly by a complete change of your mind. Then you will be able to know the will of God—what is good and is pleasing to him and is perfect.

One thing becomes very clear from this. Worship isn't something confined to an hour on Sunday morning. Our worship is the offering of the whole of our life to God.

> *Praise the Lord!*
> *Sing a new song to the Lord;*
> *praise him in the assembly of his*
> *faithful people!*
> *Be glad, Israel, because of your*
> *Creator;*
> *rejoice, people of Zion, because of*
> *your King!*
> *Praise his name with dancing;*
> *play drums and harps in praise of*
> *him.*
>
> PSALM 149

LET'S HEAR IT FOR GOD!

Perhaps when someone urges us to praise God, our minds go blank, our hearts feel like lead, and our lips are sealed.

It is here that the Bible is invaluable, for it opens up many vistas of praise.

First and foremost, we praise God for himself.

For who he is.

Come, let us praise the Lord!
Let us sing for joy to God, who
*   protects us!*
Let us come before him with
*   thanksgiving*
and sing joyful songs of praise.
for the Lord is a mighty God,
a mighty king over all the gods.
    Psalm 95

We can praise God for the great things he's done.

When we stand back from our clutter of plastic cups and microchips and look again at the vastness and beauty of creation, then wonder and praise well up in our hearts:

No one helped God spread out the
heavens or trample the sea-monster's
back. God hung the stars in the sky—
the Great Bear, Orion, the Pleiades,
and the stars of the south. We cannot
understand the great things he does,
and of his miracles there is no end.
    The book of Job

They cried to the Lord in their trouble,
    and he delivered them from their
        distress;
He made the storm be still;
    and the waves of the sea were
        hushed.
Then they were glad because they
        had quiet,
    and he brought them to their
        desired haven.
Let them thank the Lord for his stead-
        fast love,
    for his wonderful works to
        humankind.

PSALM 107

67

Praising God isn't something confined to church worship—we can praise and thank God wherever we are, whatever we are doing

God may be invisible, but the evidence of his creativity is all around us and we praise him for it:

Our Lord and God! You are worthy to receive glory, honour, and power. For you created all things, and by your will they were given existence and life.

The Revelation of John

It's a sobering thought—sobering but exciting—that human beings are the only creatures in the world that can bless God. A young lamb can enjoy the sensations of spring, but it doesn't marvel at the view or take photos of the daffodils. An owl may hunt by moonlight, but would never concern itself with sending a space probe to Mars. And this is because humans are different. We have a capacity to observe, investigate and admire. And with our ability to wonder goes the privilege of praise.

We can praise God for reaching out to us.

He hasn't left us alone and in the dark to puzzle out our identity and discover our whereabouts. He's made himself known—in general through his work in creation, and in particular through his word in the Bible.

The Jews saw God's law as their greatest treasure. It was—and is—so manifestly true. As we delve into God's word, the Bible, we see how everything hangs together. It fits. It works. And if we take it to heart and obey it, God's law becomes for us the path of freedom. As the Psalmist puts it:

The law of the Lord is perfect;
it gives new strength.
The commands of the Lord are
    trustworthy,
giving wisdom to those who lack it.
The laws of the Lord are right,

and those who obey them are happy.
The commands of the Lord are just
and give understanding to the mind.

Psalm 19

God's word is in every sense a revelation. It opens up for us the truth about God, about our world and about ourselves. And so we praise God for his revealed truth.

We praise God for rescuing us.

He rescued the Jews. They could never forget that they were a rescued people. When they'd sunk deep into Egyptian slavery, God rescued them against all the odds. And their deliverance was very little to do with Moses—in fact he doesn't get a mention in the Passover celebration even today. The exodus from Egypt and the birth of the nation of Israel were due solely to the majestic intervention of Almighty God.

For Christians, there's been a greater and more recent exodus. Through his death on the cross, Jesus won for us a glorious victory over sin and death, and opened up the way home to God.

We can never praise God enough for giving his only Son to be our Saviour—but we can make a start with Peter's words:

Let us give thanks to the God and
Father of our Lord Jesus Christ!
Because of his great mercy he gave us
new life by raising Jesus Christ from
death.

We praise God for his dealings with us.

All the reasons for praise we've spoken of apply to everyone else as much as to ourselves. But we can pause and count our own blessings. On the spur of the moment, we can't think of any. And then we realize that there are one or two—and after that the number begins to escalate quite quickly.

When we look at all that God has given us. When we consider the way he's provided for us and the distance he's brought us ... When our eyes are opened and we realize, perhaps for the first time, the amazing difference God has made to our lives, then we can say with the Psalmist:

You have done many things for us,
*   O Lord our God;*
there is no one like you!
You have made many wonderful
*   plans for us.*
I could never speak of them all—
their number is so great!

Psalm 40

69

A mother's joy

The Lord has filled my heart with joy; how happy I am because of what he has done! I laugh at my enemies; how joyful I am because God has helped me! No one is holy like the Lord; there is none like him, no protector like our God.

HANNAH'S PRAYER WHEN SHE DEDICATED HER SON SAMUEL TO GOD

Palms down, palms up

A simple exercise, involving some action, is described by Richard Foster. He calls it 'palms down, palms up'.

Begin by placing your palms down as a symbolic indication of your desire to turn over any concerns you may have to God. Inwardly you may pray, 'Lord, I give to you my anger toward John. I release my fear of my dentist appointment this morning. I surrender my anxiety over not having enough money to pay the bills this month. I release my frustration over trying to find a babysitter for tonight.' Whatever it is that weighs on your mind or is a concern to you, just say, 'Palms down'. Release it. You may even feel a certain sense of release in your hands.

After several moments of surrender, turn your palms up as a symbol of

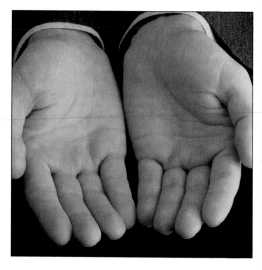

your desire to receive from the Lord. Perhaps you will pray silently: 'Lord, I would like to receive your divine love for John, your peace about the dentist appointment, your patience, your joy.' Whatever you need, you say, 'Palms up'.

Having 'centred down', spend the remaining moments in complete silence. Do not ask for anything. Allow the Lord to commune with your spirit, to love you. If impressions or directions come, fine; if not, fine.

Too many Christians rely on a 'secondhand' relationship with God. They trade blessed thoughts picked up from other people's devotions, or relay half-digested principles passed on by a friend of a friend who read it in a book or heard it on tape. But when we spend time with God by ourselves, we're embarking on our own unique adventure. Friends and books and tapes are all very well, but they're a poor substitute for the privilege of coming into God's presence ourselves. That's telling it straight! But it's the only way. If we're angry with God, we must tell him so. If we're bored, we must confess that too. Unless we learn to locate our real selves, and express ourselves as we are to God as he is, we can never enter fully into prayer.

REMEMBERING TO SAY THANK YOU

Most of us can get quite good at asking God for things, but do we always remember to thank him? Too often we're like spoilt children at Christmas—so busy opening the next parcel that we don't think to say thank you for the gift we've just opened and pushed to one side.

The apostle Paul encouraged the Christians at Thessalonia to thank God, not just for specific gifts, but for the whole context of our lives:

Be joyful always, pray at all times, be thankful in all circumstances. This is what God wants from you in your life in union with Christ Jesus.

Paul's emphasis is on thanking God that he knows all about our situation, even when we long for our circumstances to improve. And this was something Paul and his companion Silas had practised themselves, when they'd been arrested, beaten and thrown into prison in Philippi. At midnight, despite their bleeding backs and the darkness and stench of the cell, they prayed and sang hymns to God.

And may the same be true when we go through the difficult times which can come to us all— bereavement, unemployment, illness or disgrace. We can hardly thank God for any of these things in themselves but, as the Psalmist knew, we can thank him that he knows where we are, and that he cares about every detail of our lives:

I waited patiently for the Lord's help; then he listened to me and heard my cry.
He pulled me out of a dangerous pit, out of the deadly quicksand.
He set me safely on a rock and made me secure.
He taught me to sing a new song, a song of praise to our God.

All my being, praise

Praise the Lord, my soul!
  All my being, praise his holy name!
Praise the Lord, my soul,
  and do not forget how kind he is.
He forgives all my sins
  and heals all my diseases.
He keeps me from the grave
  and blesses me with love and mercy.
He fills my life with good things,
  so that I stay young and strong like an eagle.

PSALM 103

When we learn to be quiet with God, we find the secret of re-creation. We find ourselves renewed and refreshed

Getting ready to pray

Most of us need to prepare for prayer.

Muslims have always recognized this, and they precede their prayer times with careful ritual washing.

For Christians, the important advice comes from Jesus, to go to your room, close the door, and pray to your Father, who is unseen. But our room itself may prove a distraction if there's a pile of dishwashing to be done, some post to be opened, or a television to be flicked on . . .

So we must learn to know ourselves! We may need to tidy the room the night before, and open our Bible at the psalm we plan to read. We must learn to ignore the person whistling in the street outside, and resist the impulse to make the call we put off yesterday.

All this is part of 'pulling ourselves together' in the presence of God, ready to wait on him—and no doubt we'll often fail. At the same time, when genuine interruptions come, we must accept them with patience and love. If our prayer time is broken by the children waking earlier than usual, then our worship must take the form of caring for the little ones God has given us, and praising him for the wonder of family life. When they're old enough to understand, you can tell them what you're doing, and ask them to help by allowing you some quiet time. John Wesley's mother, Susannah, had nineteen children, all of whom knew that when she pulled her apron over her face, she was praying.

Where there's a will, there's a way!

WAITING FOR GOD

What about the times when nothing much seems to be going on? When the thing we're asking God for hasn't yet happened?

The Bible has a lot to say about 'waiting'.

Do we hang about with time on our hands, helpless and listless? Or are we alert, watchful and excited, as when we stand on the platform to greet an old friend, or when we're going to a party in half an hour?

The Bible says that waiting is a sign of trust:

'Those who trust in the Lord for help will find their strength renewed,' finds the prophet Isaiah.

We learn to be silent in his presence, letting the storm of our busyness blow itself out. As the psalmist relates, 'I wait patiently for God to save me; I depend on him alone.'

The prophet Elijah had this experience when he met with God on Mount Sinai. He'd come straight to Sinai after a titanic struggle with the prophets of Baal on Mount Carmel, at the end of which God had revealed himself in awesome power by sending fire from heaven.

No doubt Elijah, being something of a fiery character himself, expected further pyrotechnics from God. After all, it was on Sinai that God had given Moses the Law, and on that occasion the landscape had been covered with smoke, the Lord had been present like a furnace, and the air had been filled with thunder and a crescendo of trumpeting.

As Elijah waited for God to show himself, he experienced a furious whirlwind, followed by an earthquake and then a fire. But the Lord was not in any of them. And then the Bible says that 'after the

Sometimes we feel as if God can't hear us, that our prayers are not being answered. We have to trust that God is there and patiently wait for him to do his work in his own time

fire, there was the soft whisper of a voice'. And when Elijah heard this, he covered his face with his cloak and emerged from his cave to stand in the presence of the Lord.

We must be careful not to dictate the way in which the Lord will make himself known to us. We must abandon any idea of telling him what he must do. Instead, we must let God be God, and patiently wait for the Lord to do his work in his own time.

But waiting can also mean being tense and stretched

This is not at all a passive notion. Sometimes when we wait for God, we're really hanging on. In fact a word which normally means 'a rope' is sometimes used in the Bible to mean 'hope', as it does here in the Psalms: 'Lord, I put my hope in you; I have trusted in you since I was young.'

Elsewhere in the Psalms, this kind of waiting is likened to the eagerness of the night watchman who looks out for signs of the dawn:

*I wait eagerly for the Lord's help,
and in his word I trust.
I wait for the Lord
more eagerly than watchmen wait
    for the dawn.*

Or we can be 'waiting' like those who are doing their duty or standing in attendance.

This is a most important attitude of prayer, and we find Abraham standing before God in this way as he pleads for the evil city of Sodom

to be spared. The great prophet Samuel was like this too, standing between God and the people asking God to spare them from the judgment they deserved.

If we are the kind of people who agonize about the state of the world, or 'wonder what things are coming to', then this is the kind of prayer for us. We can turn our God-given sensitivity into heartfelt prayer, that God will act in mercy and not in judgment.

The final (and most exciting) aspect of 'waiting' is that we know we're waiting for God to do something wonderful, and that we won't wait in vain.

Noah waited in this way after the dove had returned to the ark with a fresh olive leaf in its beak. He knew that the water-level was going down, and that the flood would soon be over. Today he would wait with a smile and tell reporters, 'We're winning!'

In the New Testament, we find the beggar at the Beautiful Gate looking up at Peter and John with the same expression. He knows that something is about to happen, and that when it happens it'll be good.

So when 'nothing much is going on', we still have every reason to be in good heart. When we're waiting for God, there's no room for apathy or despondency. Rather we confidently expect his healing, justice, deliverance—whatever. He hasn't deserted us. He hasn't lost interest. He hasn't gone to sleep.

Let's make sure we don't either!

PRAYER PRACTICALITIES

A prayer list or calendar can be a great help—but revise it frequently! A prayer list in particular is supposed to be a servant rather than a master. It is to remind you that you want to pray for a particular person or situation each day, or on a particular day in the week or month.

Pray for people as you meet them in the street or at work.

Pray before you lift the receiver to answer the telephone, or as you go to open the door.

Luke's Gospel says that Jesus told his disciples to talk to the houses! 'Whenever you go into a house, first say, "Peace be with this house." '

By this he meant that whenever we go in his name we take his peace—the health and harmony of God himself. And as we're conscious of taking God's blessing with us, we become more positive and sensitive in our attitude to people.

Some people like to keep a prayer diary or journal. In it they make a note of any particular promise or prompting that seems to be from God. They also note particular prayer requests—and on the opposite page they record the answers. It's quite amazing to see how God has blessed us with answers to prayer—by overruling difficult situations, by turning

enemies into friends, by providing daily needs.

Some people like to keep birthdays and anniversaries as special days of prayer. One eighteenth-century man of God used to make his birthday a day of humble prayer and self-searching.

If we live in a state of constant busyness, it's good to plan a few days away in peace and quiet at least once a year. This isn't to be confused with holiday, and is better called a 'retreat'! Perhaps with a quiet house or room to stay in, and

When prayer becomes part of all we do and experience, we begin to see people and events in a different light. We can develop the habit of praying for those around us each day

with beautiful surroundings, we can allow God to refresh us through the peace and loveliness of his creation. Take your Bible with you and enjoy one or two of the Psalms—but be kind to yourself and pack some novels as well.

Get to know some short prayers which you can use anywhere at any time. The fourteenth-century author of *The Cloud of Unknowing* taught that 'the short prayer pierceth heaven'. We can develop our own favourite phrases for use as we walk along, or drive the car, or do the dish-washing. Just one word may be enough: 'Father!' or 'Jesus!' One very famous prayer, actually called the 'Jesus prayer', is simply, 'Lord Jesus Christ, have mercy on me'. Only a few words, but many experienced Christians have spent their lives exploring its depths.

Develop the habit of praying instinctively when certain sights and sounds present themselves. Pray for the people you take for granted each day—the ticket-collector, the milkman, the cashier at the checkout. When you hear the

Partners in prayer

Praying together should be one of the greatest privileges of married life, but it can prove very hard to get around to. There may be difficulties in finding a suitable time, or in the style of prayer that each prefers. There may be a problem of leadership, with one partner expected to take the initiative in suggesting prayer—and then to do all the praying. It may even happen that praying together goes sour and turns into getting at each other in front of God.

If this is you, then take heart! Christian couples are in fact praying together a lot—although by no means always do they pray about the same thing in the same words in the same place and at the same time.

As with so many other aspects of marriage, we must accept each other as we really are, and not spend our time and energy trying to redesign the partner God has given us!

John Richards suggests a simple way forward, which he

describes as 'a one-minute four-point programme'. It runs as follows:

- **Agree a time to pray**
A time which is signalled not by one partner calling the other, but by an independent source such as the oven timer, an alarm watch, a chiming clock, or the end of a meal or TV programme.

- **Be natural**
Sit or kneel—whichever you prefer. Hold hands or share a book if that helps express your togetherness.

- **Make peace**
Say to each other: 'The peace of the Lord be always with you,' 'And also with you.'

- **Share a short silence for your own quiet prayer**
This avoids the pressure (or embarrassment) of putting deep thoughts into words; or risking an action replay of a family row.

- **Say the Lord's Prayer together**
And that's it!

Of course, you can build on this structure in any way you both agree—by including a short psalm or other Bible reading, by listening to music or a tape, by including a confession or a prayer from a prayer book . . . But keep it simple, keep it short.

THE SMALL GROUP

Many of us find it easier to pray with one or two others. Somehow it helps us locate and define what we really want to pray about. It encourages us to be specific in our faith, and to discern together what God wants of us in our particular situation.

Of course, we may be reluctant to get involved in a prayer meeting if we're afraid it will be an over-intense experience. For this reason, we must be secure in our friendship if we're meeting with one or two others, and have confidence in the leader if the group is any larger.

We may also be afraid that we have nothing to say! One way round this is to go along with part of a psalm to read to the others, or a short episode from the Bible which has been striking you as fresh and relevant. You can also decide together to keep prayers short—perhaps just a single sentence—and not to be afraid of the silences in between. Once you're through the 'panic barrier', silence can be wonderfully relaxing and helpful. All the same, don't let it go on so long that you begin to wonder whether the others are asleep!

All the basic rules of praying on our own apply to praying together.

Praying in a small group can help us to develop a richer understanding of prayer, and it can offer mutual support and encouragement too

Asking for healing

At some time in our life we're bound to ask God for healing—if not for ourselves, then for others.

When we're experiencing pain, depression or tension—or when we are in the presence of someone else's suffering—we long for God to help. Operations, injections, pills and counselling all have their place. But physical help is always limited, whereas spiritual help is unlimited . . .

And so we humble ourselves and turn to God.

But is it right to believe that when we sincerely pray for healing, our aches and pains will disappear; our rashes and swellings and growths will vanish?

It's certainly true that God can do anything. If he's the one who created the universe, who sustains it to this day, and who by his mighty power raised Jesus from death, then he's surely able to reach out to all who suffer in body, mind or spirit. Many of us have experienced such healing in our own lives,

or have had the privilege of seeing it in the lives of others.

But the stark truth is that while some are healed, many others continue to suffer. And even those who are cured of depressions, diseases or deformities may still fall ill again in due course and will certainly die eventually, albeit of old age.

While it's the most natural thing in the world to ask God for healing (and we all need healing in any number of ways), the truth is that none of us will experience perfect wholeness in this life. If we cling to a formula that 'all we have to do is ask, and we shall be healed', we open wide the door to heartache, guilt and despair. We're bound to wonder what sin or lack of faith is blocking our recovery. We may be tempted to pretend that our illness has gone away—or put others under pressure to spring from their wheelchairs or flush away their tablets.

In fact the right way to pray for healing is to begin by asking God

what he wants. And the answer will surely come along the line of God wanting to assure us of his presence and love. His power may be seen to best advantage in dramatic healing. If so, we praise him. On the other hand, his love may be seen in a real and deep way through our patience and trust—and through the care we can give and receive in our suffering.

Paul himself had to discover that pain, discomfort and inconvenience can all be transformed for the glory of God. In particular he was dogged by a painful physical ailment. He explained to the Christians at Corinth how he had come to see that it was an illness God could use to keep him from being proud:

Three times I prayed to the Lord about this and asked him to take it away. But his answer was: 'My grace is all you need, for my power is strongest when you are weak.'

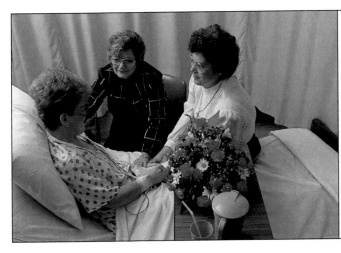

We are told in the Bible that God is able to do so much more than we can ever ask for, or even think of. So, when someone is ill, it's absolutely right to pray for him or her

a symbol of God's ability to reach out and help.

Alternatively such prayer may take place during a church service, with the church leaders and those gifted in healing gathering round to anoint and lay hands on the sick person. However prayer for healing takes place, certain ground rules will always apply:

We should always praise and thank God for his love.

We can rest in the assurance that he will do what's best.

We should be prepared to go on praying.

After all, we're not just seeking a shortcut to avoid further trips to the doctor. We're asking God by his Holy Spirit to work deeply in the lives of all those involved. This may take a lot of patient waiting on God and sensitive listening to what he has to say. There may need to be healing of memories or relationships. It may be necessary to write to somebody or visit them, to confess a wrong and to ask forgiveness. And so the healing we seek goes wider and deeper than ever we guessed when we first began to pray.

Most importantly, we mustn't presume to tell God what to do.

He is God, and he must have his way. Just because we read in a book or heard on the grapevine that someone with a particular illness was cured in a particular way, we mustn't assume that there's some magic formula to be discovered and applied. He is a creative God of infinite originality and variety, not a conveyor-belt mechanic who does the same thing the same way all the time. If we're open to him—open to his transforming power in our lives—there's no limit to the ways in which his glory can be revealed in us.

WHEN ALL IS DARK

How can we possibly pray when the worst thing in the world has happened to us?

How can we put our trust in God, or believe in him as a loving Father, when our world has come to an end—our nightmare has come true?

The only way to make any sense of tragedy is to look again at Jesus on his cross. The evils he endured were not of his making. He was on the receiving end of all that is vile in human nature—pride, fear, hypocrisy, injustice and rage.

We can add to that list our own catalogue of natural disasters, dreadful accidents and ghastly mistakes. Even within our own small circle of family and friends we know of those whose lives can never be the same again, because of some particular tragedy.

But because of what Jesus went through on the cross, and because God raised him to life in triumph, we can clearly see that suffering and death do not, and will not, have the last word.

When the worst thing in all the world happens to us, then we find ourselves very close to the heart of God. He knows what it is to suffer more than we ever can. After all, God is love—and love is constantly exposed to misunderstanding, rejection and hurt. In our own suffering, our eyes can be opened, and our compassion awakened, to Jesus who suffers for us and with

However dark the world may seem, however bleak the future looks, we can trust that God is with us in our pain and offers real hope

us. And who brings us through the long dark tunnel of anguish to life and health and peace.

92

PRAYING BIG

When we first start to pray, the likelihood is that we will be 'thinking small'.

We may have been driven to prayer by an immediate and personal need—an emergency or a scare—and we find ourselves on our knees begging God for his help.

But as our experience of prayer grows, so we can enlarge our thinking. We can pray for members of our family, or those in our circle of friends. We can ask God's blessing on the members of our church, and perhaps especially our church leaders because they're at the forefront of spiritual warfare.

But our prayers can range wider still! We can bring to God the needs of the world: the helplessness of the hungry and the poor; the frustrations of the unemployed; the agonies of those who are brokenhearted, or who suffer brutality, injustice or discrimination.

And there is no door in the world that is closed to us. Our prayers for God's blessing can range from the White House to Whitehall, and from the corridors of the Kremlin to the streets of Calcutta. There is no palace, embassy or government building in the world that is outside the range of our prayers.

Paul wrote to his friend Timothy:

First of all, then, I urge that petitions, prayers, requests, and thanksgivings be offered to God for all people; for kings and all others who are in authority, that we may live a quite and peaceful life with all reverence towards God and with proper conduct. This is good and it pleases God our Saviour, who wants everyone to be saved and to come to know the truth.

But we should note that the aim of our prayer isn't that we should win some kind of control over current affairs. Rather we're asking that every society may become the kind of environment in which the Good News of Jesus can take root and spread.

'Peace' is never, in God's reckoning, merely the absence of war. God's peace comes when people live harmoniously in obedience to his truth, when enemies are reconciled and divisions are healed. So when we pray for people who are national or international leaders, we're asking that God will help them to establish a world of justice, peace and economic stability—a world in which people may be free to hear, receive and respond to the gospel.

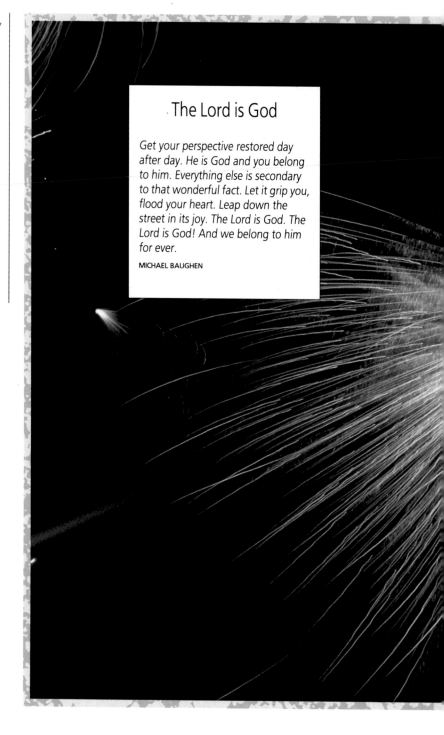

The Lord is God

Get your perspective restored day after day. He is God and you belong to him. Everything else is secondary to that wonderful fact. Let it grip you, flood your heart. Leap down the street in its joy. The Lord is God. The Lord is God! And we belong to him for ever.

MICHAEL BAUGHEN

Picture acknowledgments
Jon Arnold 71; Susanna Burton 7, 10 (centre),
27, 40, 42, 58, 68, 80/81, 87, 92; Ebenezer
Pictures (Susanna Burton) 10 (bottom);
Lion Publishing 9, 10 (top), 13, 30, 36/37, 52/53,
(CMS) 56, 65, 72; Nicholas Rous 23, 38/39, 49,
55; ZEFA 19, 70, 74, 94/95, (B.Binzen) 76/77,
(Tom Casalini) 57, (Jon Feingersh) 14,
(P.Garfield) 20, 86, (Dr D.James) 66/67, (Ronnie
Kaufman) 85, (C.Krebs) 32, (Rick McIntyre) 62/
63, (David Muench) 29, (Spectra-Action) 24/25,
(D.Stoecklein) 46/47, (Carl Tuttle) 11, 14,
(Ed Wheeler) 91, (Art Wolfe) 12/13;
Simon Zisman 78